CONFESSIONS

of an

Ex-Crossmaker

E. K. Bailey

Moody Publishers

CHICAGO

How I Met the Crossmaker

I have been preaching and pastoring for approximately forty years. My life has been consumed with the preaching and the propagation of the Gospel. There is no greater satisfaction, no comparison to the joy I experience when I preach the glorious gospel of Christ. I believe the Bible is the infallible, inerrant Word of God that transforms lives and saves people from their sins.

I have always asserted that in an ever-changing culture it is very important that preachers remain uncompromising in their commitment to preaching the Scriptures and to be relevant when they communicate the message of a text. I have attempted to remain relevant with my own congregation. And the following sermon represents my effort to contemporarize the message of the Cross without violating any of the principles of hermeneutics or homiletics just to be relevant for our day.

Confessions of an Ex-Crossmaker is a scintillating sermon about the effervescent events of Easter. I have told the story in an unusual manner—it's in first person, and I became Ben Levi in telling it to my congregation. Nevertheless, I have endeavored to remain faithful to the cultural and historical setting of the original Easter events. Though one may argue that Ben Levi is a fictional character, his character is fictional only in name.

Ben Levi is a depiction of us all, from the dawn of history to our present day. Though there are many other ways to tell this simple but supernatural life-changing story, I thought it would be effective and real to relive the passion through the eyes of an ordinary individual who was there.

And Ben Levi must have been there for someone had to make the cross on which the Prince of Glory died!

Though I don't know how my illness with cancer will end, I believe the Word of God, which I have preached to my own congregation and to thousands of people across the United States and around the world. God can heal me if He so desires—and I am praying that He will—but if He decides not to heal me, He is sovereign and I will love Him, trust Him, and worship Him still. And then, along with Ben Levi and all other ex-crossmakers, I will see Jesus and and those nail-scarred hands in heaven.

CONFESSIONS

of an
Ex-Crossmaker

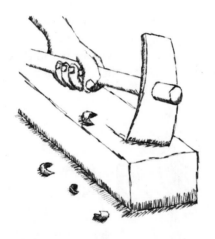

My name is Ben Levi.

I am a member of the distinguished tribe of Benjamin, which is part of the original twelve tribes of Israel.

During the Roman occupation of Palestine, I was a crossmaker.

Cross making was a thriving industry then. I made a good living in the business until that ill-fated Friday, when I was forced to face the hideous consequences of my craftsmanship. Even now sometimes, the guilt, like a tidal wave, overwhelms me.

I am the man who made the cross upon which Jesus was cruelly crucified and later died.

It is normally around the Easter celebration when I am invited all over the world to share my testimony. I dub it "The Confessions of an Ex-

Crossmaker." Not many Jews were in my line of work. The law required that one make a pledge of allegiance to Herod in order to secure a government contract to facilitate doing business with the Roman army. Those of us who became Herodians for economic reasons were looked upon by the traditionalists of our race to be, at best, guilty of treason, and, at worst, in league with the Devil.

Although profitable, it was a lonely life. So like the tax collector, the Jewish crossmaker was ostracized, stigmatized, and criticized as a reproach to the nation.

As a teenager, I never intended to become a crossmaker. I remember viewing cross making as a disgusting, death-dealing enterprise of a debased and decadent people. My parents were shepherds by trade, and in an attempt to diversify the family business, they sent me away to tailoring school to become skilled in the making and merchandising of clothes from the sheep's wool.

One summer, I was given a job at the Shalom sawmill in Jerusalem as an apprentice carpenter. The money, I thought, could be used to help pay my way through school. However, what began as a temporary internship, ended up as a permanent profession. The Jerusalem economy was booming. The demand for wood exceeded its supply. Even for an apprentice, the job was lucrative—so much so that I never went back to tailoring school.

The truth is I never did enjoy those hot sweatshops and the dull tailoring teachers. The lumberjacks of the sawmill were so much more interesting that I could hardly wait for morning to come in order to be around those older men. They were always fanning flies and telling lies. I was enthralled by their war stories, intrigued by their wounds and the tales about their wives.

EVERYONE AGREED THAT I WAS THE BEST YOUNG APPRENTICE WHO HAD EVER WORKED IN THE SAWMILL.

The hard work was rewarded as I quickly achieved upward mobility in the corporate organization.

After several years, the owner, Mr. Silverstein, was so impressed with my work that he made me a junior partner. Mr. Silverstein remarked that my creative and innovative ideas had raised the level of productivity and revenue, which brought significant profit to the company. Thus, I was catapulted to second in command. Not long thereafter, Mr. Silverstein suddenly died, and unfortunately he had no heirs. His two sons died in an earlier revolt against the Romans that was led by Tudas and Judas of Galilee. It was only one year later that his wife died of a broken heart.

To say that I was shocked is to put it mildly, when the executor of the estate told me that Mr. Silverstein had bequeathed his lucrative business to me. After making a few changes, the business became one of the top moneymaking businesses in the nation of Israel. Shortly thereafter I was elected president of the local chamber of commerce.

THEN CAME THE RECESSION.

It lasted much longer than economists had predicted. Many people lost jobs; some lost homes, and there were those who lost everything. As I teetered on the edge of bankruptcy, I became more a man of desperation.

Whether it was out of the blue or by divine intervention, a Roman soldier offered to buy all my lumber. He explained that there had been a major insurrection up in Nazareth. He said that the Romans needed two thousand crosses immediately. He asked how many crosses I could quickly supply him with.

Of course, I knew what it would mean if I signed those papers, but not to sign the contract meant losing everything. . . .

SO, QUICKLY I PUT MY NAME ON THE
DOTTED LINE.

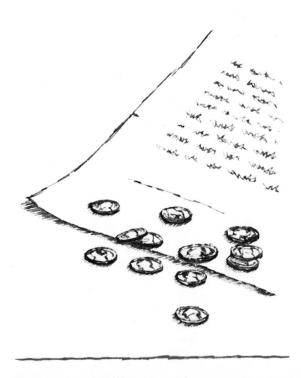

Immediately, both joy and sorrow began to mingle in my heart. The joy was there because finally I was able to funnel some much needed revenue into my sagging business. The sorrow was there because I knew that somehow I had sold my soul to the Romans for a pile of lumber.

Do you understand my predicament? Do you see where I was? I had to feed my family. It was the only way we would survive.

Oh, I know, I am rationalizing again. At first, I thought that I would make the crosses just until the economy recovered, but the recovery never came. I was stuck in the predicament of being the supplier of crosses to the Roman government.

How much do you know about the Romans?

Simply stated, their empire lasted nearly five hundred years. Their impressive boundaries stretched from the Ganges River in India all the way to the shores of the British Isles. Their invincible army conquered Assyria to the north and Babylon to the south. My nation, Palestine, was the tiny peninsula that linked those two great nations.

None of us was a match for the military prowess of the Roman army. We were all devoured like a flock of locusts on a field; the army left only death and destruction lying in its wake.

THE ROMANS WERE INEXPRESSIBLY CRUEL AND RUTHLESS IN THEIR ENFORCEMENT OF ROMAN LAW.

If one dared speak against their insane emperor or the insidious laws of the infamous Herod, he could easily end up on one of my crosses.

I witnessed so many crucifixions that my senses were dulled to their agony and wretchedness. The criminals who died on those crosses became a part of the Jerusalem landscape. I reasoned that it was an ugly business but someone had to do it. *I didn't create this evil system. Therefore, I am not responsible for the deaths of those who hung on the crosses. The Romans pay me to make the crosses,* I told myself, *and make crosses I do.*

Crosses were not difficult to make.

I would simply use my saw to cut the trees into upright beams and shorter crosspieces. Next I would fasten the two beams together so that the upright beam projected above the shorter crosspiece.

On the good crosses, I would install a saddle. I would cut out a hole approximately four by six inches in the upright beam and then insert a piece of wood, upon which the criminal sat. The saddle served several purposes. It would help to hold the criminal on the cross as he was lifted up. It would also prevent the criminal's hands from literally tearing away from the cross. The saddle also prolonged the crucifixion process. Those were my best crosses.

Whenever I had a large order, I made the cheaper kind. They were simple to make because crossbeams just sat on a peg on top of the uprights. The cheap crosses could be used only once. Then they had to be burned or thrown away; but the Romans would wash down the good crosses and use them over and over again.

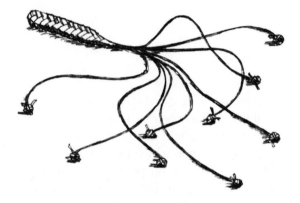

Prior to any criminal being nailed, he received the scourging. The scourging helped him to die quicker. The Romans would employ the biggest, meanest, and strongest soldier they could find. The soldier would get a long whip, called the scourge, that had leather straps tied around pieces of broken bones, jagged stones, and sharp metal. The flogging was limited to thirty-nine stripes—two-thirds across the back and one-third across the chest. The metal, stone, and bones would literally tear the flesh of the criminal's body, leaving his back a bloody mess.

SOME MEN NEVER MADE
IT TO THE CROSS. THEY
DIED AS A RESULT OF THE
SCOURGING.

Once a year, the Romans made a futile attempt at being civilized. During the annual celebration of the Passover, more than three million Jews crowded into the city. Passover was a time that we Jews commemorated our deliverance out of Egyptian slavery. Not wanting to incite a riot, the Romans would attempt to appease the Jews by releasing a political prisoner.

THAT YEAR THEY CRIED FOR THE RELEASE OF BARABBAS, AND FOR JESUS TO BE CRUCIFIED!

It was late that Thursday evening, long after my family had settled into bed, that a ferocious knock awakened the whole house. A loud and angry voice shouted,

"Levi, Levi, open in the name of the Roman government!"

With fear gripping my heart, I quickly slipped on my tunic. I knew that if a centurion was at my door at that hour, there certainly had to be trouble in the air. I could only hope that it was business he wanted and that I was not the object of his anger.

The centurion told me that a trial was in progress. I dared not ask whose trial, although it did cross my mind that night trials were illegal. The centurion told me that it did not look good for the wretched soul, and he was fairly certain that there would be a crucifixion on Friday. I asked him if there was only one man, why did they need three crosses. The centurion told me that there were two thieves who had already been found guilty and sentenced to death.

"I've already made two crosses."

"That may be, but I want one of the crosses to be one of your good ones."

"Yes, yes," I assured him. "I will stay up through the night, and you shall have your crosses by seven o'clock Friday morning."

Long before the sun rose that Friday, I had delivered the three crosses to Antonio's fortress, adjacent to the temple area. Exhausted from the work and lack of sleep, I decided not to open for business that day. After all, it was Passover. Although, I wasn't much of a religious Jew, I respected the Sabbath. So, after returning home and eating my usual meal of fish and unleavened bread, I joined the throng of people who had made their way to the Holy City to celebrate Passover.

The city was alive. The beggars were intoning "Alms for the poor!" The hawkers were selling their wares. The priests were chanting their religious songs. The people were bantering in the streets. The cacophony of the crowd was everywhere.

As I elbowed my way through the jostling crowd, I came upon a caravan of criminals who were surrounded by an angry mob. This crowd was more rowdy than most crucifixion crowds.

They were jeering, spitting, cursing, and shaking their fists.

IT ALL SEEMED TO HAVE BEEN DIRECTED TOWARD THE ONE THEY CALLED JESUS.

As I looked closer, I could tell that He had been terribly beaten. A wreath of thorn branches was imbedded in His skull. His head and hair were caked with blood. His clothes stuck to His back, and one of my crosses weighed heavily on His shoulders. Yes, I recognized it.

The crowd did not seem satisfied; His presence seemed to draw venom from their pores.

As the crossbearers stumbled through the narrow streets, the one called Jesus fell near where I was standing. Something within me yearned to help, but my desire was held in check by my knowledge of Roman brutality. As Jesus struggled to His feet, His eyes met mine.

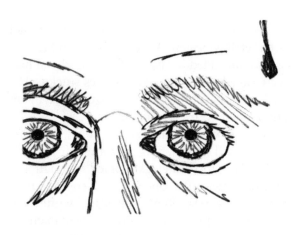

I HAD NEVER BEEN SO CAPTIVATED
BY A SIMPLE LOOK—A LOOK OF
QUIET STRENGTH.

His eyes reflected a profound peace, while His flesh endured unbridled castigation. His body seemed shrunken. His shoulders weighted down with pain.

ALTHOUGH HE WAS BEING DRIVEN TO THE HILL OF CRUCIFIXION, SOMETHING ABOUT HIS DEMEANOR DEMONSTRATED HE WAS IN CONTROL OF HIS PRESENT PREDICAMENT.

This was a strange and unexpected conclusion for the man who on Palm Sunday had swung around the brow of Olivet amid the antiphonal cries of "Hosanna!" His entry into Jerusalem, the city of David, had been triumphal. Now, that event seemed so long ago.

Though my contact with Him had been impersonal and brief, I could see why so many people had been drawn to Him. His countenance had a compelling, gripping power. I slowly began to understand why the people thought that He could save them. There was something about Him—a fascinating, mysterious presence.

A soldier quickly pressed the point of his sword into the side of a startled bystander and compelled him to help carry the cross. Later, many of us learned that the man was Simon of Cyrene. Simon was an elegant looking black man from a small town in northern Africa, who would eventually become a leader in a movement and father of two outstanding preachers. The same soldier then pressed the caravan into motion.

As the caravan slowly weaved its way through the narrow streets of Jerusalem, angry faces watched the three men stagger toward their final destiny. I cannot explain why I followed this strange sampling of human society.

The Roman soldiers were there, in the midst of that human caravan. Their heartlessness seemed to have been heightened because of the miserable conditions in this fly-infested, sweltering wasteland somewhere on the backside of the Roman Empire. The curiosity seekers were also there, those who took their sport wherever they could find it. And there were the priests and temple officers. Their primary concern was to guard their vested interest, which was authority over the people. There was an odd little cluster of frightened men and women there too, but they followed from afar.

As I perused the faces, I noticed that we had gone beyond the city walls.

THAT'S WHEN I SAW THEM!

It was as if they rose up out of the ground, silhouetted against the golden backdrop of the morning sky.

THERE WERE THREE LARGE VERTICAL BEAMS LOOMING LARGE ATOP THE HILL OF THE SKULL.

The command was given for all prisoners to lie down. Quickly their naked shoulders were pinned against the rugged crossbeams. Their arms were spread to full length.

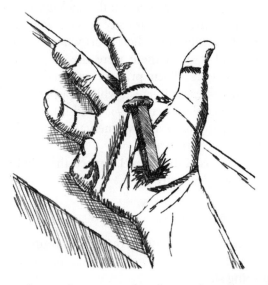

I focused on Jesus, the object of much wrath. It was His right hand that first felt the sharp prick of the nail, and at the ringing of the hammer the blood spattered and the beam splintered. His hand became a ball of fire as it was fastened against the plank. The left hand also soon exploded into fire.

His lungs were heaving. His face paled from the pain.

The soldier took His feet and pushed one atop the other. Suddenly a nail shot though one heel bone into the other. No description can do justice to the agony in His face.

The high priest began to mock Him, saying, "You saved others. Now come down and save Yourself." One of the soldiers cried, "Yes, if You're a king, come down, and we will believe You."

That's when I first heard it! That cry—

"FATHER, FORGIVE
THEM, FOR THEY
KNOW NOT WHAT
THEY DO."

I wanted to cry out to Him, "No, no, don't forgive them. The Romans don't deserve to be forgiven. Curse them back. Spit back upon them. Be defiant until the end." Hatred and resentment began to well up in my heart.

My eyes were riveted on Him. I had never witnessed innocence and wisdom so uniquely wedded together. Usually either one was wise from experience and, therefore, not innocent; or one was foolish and, therefore, not wise.

I COULD NO LONGER LOOK.

There was something about Him that con-jured up things about me that I had long since forgotten. It was like all of my past sins began to parade across the stage of my memory, and the face of every man who had died on one of my crosses had somehow been etched in my mind. Out of the murky slime of my subconscious, I heard them all crying, "Death to the crossmak-er! Death to the crossmaker!"

I wanted to run, but my feet would not move. I felt stripped and exposed. The condem-nation felt torrid, like a raging fire in my belly.

Suddenly the two malefactors, one on either side of Jesus, began to verbally attack each another. Then the one on the left side turned against Jesus. "Some Christ You turned out to be! You dared raise our hope. You enticed us to believe that You would throw off the Roman yoke, but look at You now, nailed to a cross between two thieves. I suppose this is the just end to a ludicrous dream."

The thief on the right was already appalled at his companion's blasphemous idiocy. He said, "Hold your tongue, you thieving snake. Don't you fear God? We are guilty and deserve our punishment, but this man has done no wrong."

Then, looking at the dying Jesus, he said, "Lord, I believe. Remember me when You come into Your kingdom."

His words of faith caused Jesus to rally momentarily, at least enough to say, "Today you shall be with Me in Paradise."

Later, Simon Peter explained to me that on those three crosses,

THE MAN ON THE LEFT
DIED *in* SIN.

AND THE MAN ON THE RIGHT
DIED *to* SIN.

BUT THE ONE ON THE MIDDLE CROSS
DIED *for* SIN.

Suddenly, the sun disappeared. Someone said that it was an eclipse. The air grew increasingly heavy until it was hard to breathe. The midnight darkness came at midday and draped itself like a shawl around the shoulders of Golgotha. The ground began to reel and rock like a drunken man. The earth was quaking as though it were having a seizure.

Some time passed, and then I heard Jesus cry out, "Father, into Thy hands I commend My spirit." And He bowed His head.

As I turned to run, a voice was heard above all others, exclaiming,

"SURELY THIS WAS THE SON OF GOD!"

Hoping against hope, I just said, "Surely not. This man could not have been the Son of God; He was just a good man, but not the awaited Messiah. If He, in fact, was the Son of God . . . oh, what a wretched man I am!"

"COULD IT BE
THAT I MADE
THE CROSS
ON WHICH
THE PRINCE
OF GLORY
DIED?"

Finally, I was relieved of my paralysis and able to move. I ran faster and faster, but I could not outrun my deep sense of guilt.

I WEPT BITTERLY, BUT MY TEARS COULD NOT WASH AWAY MY SIN.

I shut the door of my house, but I could not shut out the agony that apprehended my soul.

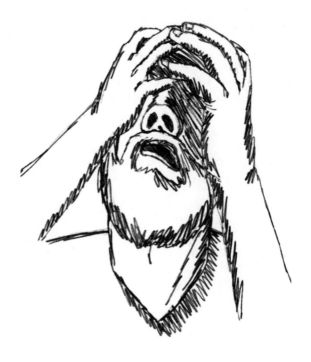

I WENT TO BED, BUT SLEEP WOULD NOT
DROWN OUT MY AGONY.

I spent the rest of that Friday rehearsing the tragic events of that last week. I tried to comprehend the enigma of the Cross. After pondering the question deep into the night, I concluded that what had taken place on that cross was beyond my comprehension. I knew that I had made the cross and that Jesus had died on the cross I made, but its meaning eluded my understanding.

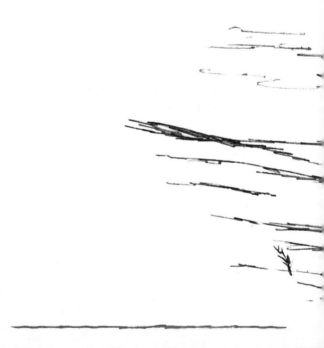

Saturday was a day of torment. Friday had shown the evil in the human heart, but Saturday showed the hopelessness of the human predicament. Friday was a day of shattered dreams and blasted hopes, but Saturday was a day without God. At least, on Friday, we had Jesus half a day, but Saturday He was dead all day long. It seemed that this dreadful day would never pass.

Mercifully, Sunday came. "What a difference a day makes!" The sounds of Sunday morning were no ordinary street noises. There was a constrained excitement in the air. People spoke in soft, hushed tones. I begged them to tell me the source of the commotion.

The first report I heard was that some women had been detained because of an empty grave. The next thing I heard was that they were looking for the disciples to charge them with grave robbing. While yet a distance from the graveyard, I heard an elderly man say,

"HE IS RISEN AS HE SAID."

Immediately reason attempted to disqualify the news. *At best, this is a conspiracy; at worst, it is a hoax,* I told myself, but there was something within me that wanted to believe. My unconverted faith said, "Keep putting one foot in front of the other."

Inside the graveyard, the soldiers would not allow us to get close to where they had laid Him, but the women testified that when they arrived to embalm His body, the stone had been rolled away and an angel sitting on the stone said to them, "Why do you look here for the living among the dead? He is not here. He has risen, as He said He would."

Hearing about the Resurrection *almost* brought me joy. I felt great hope that perhaps Jesus was the Son of God who conquered death. Yet I also felt I was living a never-ending nightmare. I did not know if God would be angry with me for making the cross or if the Resurrection had wiped the slate clean.

Then, fifty days after Easter, Peter and the remaining disciples were courageously preaching Christ in the temple area. A multitude from all over the world was confounded because every man heard the disciples speaking in their own language.

For me, the turning point came when Peter said, "Jesus of Nazareth, whom God had raised up. . . ." I could no longer hold my peace. In the middle of his sermon I asked,

"HOW DO YOU KNOW THAT THIS JESUS

WAS THE HOLY ONE OF GOD?"

Before Peter could speak,

I WAS BOMBARDED WITH THE TESTIMONIES OF PEOPLE WHO WERE THE RECIPIENTS OF HIS MIRACLES.

The widow of Nain was there. She testified how Jesus had stopped the funeral procession and gave life back to her dead son. The couple that was married at Cana were there. They testified about when the wine ran out at their wedding how Jesus had them pour in water and pour out wine. Legion was there. He testified how he used to live in the graveyard, and that Jesus had cast the demons out of his life.

The invalid man who had been at the pool for thirty and eight years also was there. He told about the many times others had stepped into the pool before him and how Jesus asked him, "Would thou be made whole?"

Bartemaeus was there too. He testified how he had been blind all of his life, and that Jesus had given sight to his blind eyes.

I said to Simon Peter, "All of these testimonies attest to His greatness while He lived, but. . . ."

Peter stopped me and said, "But He lives today!"

It was difficult for me to believe it when they said they saw Him, touched Him, and ate with Him, and that more than five hundred people had seen Him since the Resurrection.

I asked Peter if there was any hope for me. "Can I be forgiven? Would God have mercy on the man who made the cross upon which the Prince of Glory died?"

My heart leaped for joy when Peter said, "Though your sins be as scarlet, they shall be whiter than snow."

I should not be the only happy person today because I am not the only crossmaker here.

EVERY LIAR IS A CROSSMAKER.

EVERY THIEF IS A CROSSMAKER.

EVERY FORNICATOR IS A CROSSMAKER.

EVERY ADULTERER IS A CROSSMAKER.

EVERY HOMOSEXUAL IS A CROSSMAKER.

EVERY LESBIAN IS A CROSSMAKER.

EVERY PROUD HEART IS A CROSSMAKER.

EVERY REVILER IS A CROSSMAKER.

But the good news of the Gospel is that you too can be an ex-crossmaker. You don't have to be a crossmaker—you can be a crossbearer.

Jesus said,

"IF YOU WILL CONFESS YOUR SINS, I AM
FAITHFUL AND JUST TO FORGIVE YOU AND TO
CLEANSE YOU FROM ALL UNRIGHTEOUSNESS."

About the Author

E. K. Bailey (D.Min., United Theological Seminary) established the Concord Missionary Baptist Church in Dallas, Texas, in 1975. He desires to enable change for the disenfranchised, and founded E. K. Bailey Ministries, Inc. to facilitate several conferences toward this end, including the Institute on Church Growth. Dr. Bailey currently serves as the senior pastor of Concrd Missionary Baptist Church. He and his wife, Sheila, live in Dallas, Texas.

Since 1894, Moody Publishers has been dedicated to equip and motivate people to advance the cause of Christ by publishing evangelical Christian literature and other media for all ages, around the world. Because we are a ministry of the Moody Bible Institute of Chicago, a portion of the proceeds from the sale of this book go to train the next generation of Christian leaders.

If we may serve you in any way in your spiritual journey toward understanding Christ and the Christian life, please contact us at www.moodypublishers.com.

"All Scripture is God-breathed and is useful for teaching, rebuking, correcting and training in righteousness, so that the man of God may be thoroughly equipped for every good work."
—*2 TIMOTHY 3:16, 17*

MOODY
PUBLISHERS

THE NAME YOU CAN TRUST®